Tango
FOR
GUITAR
PLAYED BY BRIAN CHAMBOULEYRON

 CD Produced, composed and arranged
by Brian Chambouleyron and Jorge Polanuer.

The author wishes to acknowledge the valuable contributions of :
Mónica Cabouli, David Cantoni, Marina Carrera, Marisú Chambouleyron.
Photos: Ernesto Critzmann and Brian Jait.

Cover Photo courtesy of Yolanda Rossi & Micheal Espinoza
Tango Instructors and Performers
www.tangosplash.com www.tangoelegant.com
Layout by David Collins
Cover Layout by Eric Peterson

ISBN-13: 978-1-57424-146-4
ISBN-10: 1-57424-146-X
SAN-683-8022

Contents & CD Track List

Play - A - Long

*Themes, (guitar and accompaniment) are recorded on CD tracks 1 to 13;
 CD track 14 is the piano tuning notes.
 CD tracks 15 to 27 are Play-A-Long only.

The following people participated in the recording:
Brian Chambouleyron: guitar
Jorge Polanuer: flute
Federico Mizrahi: piano
Edgardo Cardozo: second guitar in tracks 2, 4 and 6.
Silvio Cattáneo: second guitar in track 13
Carlos Buono: bandoneon
Oscar Gulliace: violin

Preface

The guitar is a charasteristic musical instrument in Argentine culture. Since the arrival of Spaniards to South America, it has had a key role in our folk music. Its sound has been the composers and interpreters' favorite. At present there is a broad and comprehensive catalog of songs and instrumental pieces, which encompasses early genres of the 19th century as well as the latest pop creations.

At the beginning of the 20th century (around the time of the blues), the *tango* was born in Buenos Aires: a style arising from immigration and the melting pot which was going to spread dramatically all over the world. Tango is a dance, a rhythm and a charasteristic musical color.

It is in tango where the guitar reaches a remarkable level of technical and expressive development. Today I propose an approach in the *'tanguero'* style of playing the guitar, with some pieces specially composed by Jorge Polanuer, a composer and a friend, and myself. The tangos in this book are accompanied by *valses-tango* and *milonga-tango,* similar and complementary genres also played in ballrooms.

For each piece I suggest fingering based on the criterion of economy of movements. The numbers on the notes indicate the finger with which that note must be played, and the encircled number refers to the string. There can be other ways of fingering which might be more practical for you; that being the case, feel free to modify it accordingly. There's a way to play for every instrumentalist! The pieces present different degrees of complexity; therefore, they could also make an excellent complement in learning how to play the instrument.

I hope you find this approach useful and you feel like filling yourselves with *tango.*

Enjoy it !
Brian Chambouleyron

Brian Chambouleyron

Brian Chambouleyron became a musician studying several disciplines (guitar, singing, composition, musical analysis, arrangements and orchestration). Always fascinated with popular music, he traveled to different Latin American countries to learn their traditions.

He began his professional activity as a music teacher in 1990. Teaching led to the creation of children's shows. As a composer of popular songs, he participated in the Buenos Aires' Young Artists biennial exhibition. In 1993 he went on his first professional tour to Europe, going all over France and Switzerland for two months and performing as both soloist and together with other musical bands. He also gave courses on Argentine popular music. From then on, his activities in European countries became regular.

In 1996 he was in charge of the musical direction of the successful show Recuerdos son recuerdos (which received 5 ACE awards nominations). Brian Chambouleyron was nominated for 'male revelation'. (CD Recuerdos son recuerdos – La Trastienda Records). In 1998 he participated in the show Glorias Porteñas (1998 ACE award) together with Soledad Villamil, which was given an excellent reception by the critics and the public. The show toured continuously throughout Argentina, Latin America and Europe for two years, and participated in prestigious international festivals (CD Glorias Porteñas vol. I and II – Epsa Music). Brian Chambouleyron was given the 1999 Trinidad Guevara award for 'male revelation of the year' by the Department of Culture of Buenos Aires City. In 2000 he created the show Patio de Tango with Esteban Morgado, which also had a wonderful reception at a national level, and he started a long international tour (Paris, Rome, Madrid, Barcelona, etc). (CD Patio de Tango – BAM records, Department of Culture). With his last show, Tangos, valses and Milongas, he has performed in several cultural events and toured abroad, being highly acclaimed by audiences and critics.

Brian has also composed the music for several theatre plays : "La firecilla domada" , 2004; "Pequeña historia del tango", 2002; "Granadina", 2003; ect. In 2004 recorded the CD "Chambouleyron sings Gardel", a selection of the finest compositions by Gardel, arranged by B. Ch. (Random records, Buenos Aires). In 2005 recorded the CD "Voice and Guitar", Twenty tradicional tango and argentinian popular music pieces, arranged by Chambouleyron. (Random records, Buenos Aires) on le canta a Gardel (Chambouleyron sings Gardel). This work is a selection of the finest compositions by Gardel –plus a few jewels from his songbook – recreated in an intimate and romantic atmosphere. Brian Chambouleyron can be reached at:

Baldomero F. Moreno 1714 10° 111
(1406) Buenos Aires - Argentina
Tel / Fax (54) (11) 4633 5434

e-mail: brianch@infovia.com.ar ● website: www.brianchambouleyron.com.ar

*J*orge Polanuer

Saxophone player, Flutist, Composer, Arranger, and Teacher

Received his degree as Flute Professor in 1983 at the Conservatorio Nacional de "Música Carlos Lopez Buchardo", the most prestigious institution in Argentina. He has been a member of the musical-theater group Cuatro Vientos (http://www.cuatrovientos.com.ar) since 1987. With this group, he participated in numerous international festivals, including Madrid, Lisbon, Miami, Caracas, San José de Costa Rica, and Porto Alegre, and recorded five CDs in which other renowned performers have participated: Les Luthiers, Andrés Calamaro, Chango Spasiuk, and Bob Telson.

Prior to co-founding Cuatro Vientos, he took part in various Jazz, Fusion, Classical Music, and Rock groups, among them "Los Abuelos de la Nada", and Andrés Calamaro´s band, with whom he recorded four CDs.

Jorge has also composed the music for several theater plays: "Gala", "Shakespeare´s Merry Women", "Shakespiriando", "Sinvergüenzas" (No shame), "Cuatro Vientos y el Saxo Mágico" (Cuatro Vientos and the magic sax), "Alma de Saxofón" (Saxophone Soul), and "La Tempestad" (The Storm). Available on CD. He won the "Premio ACE (Asoc. Cronistas del Espectáculo) 2000" (the most important music award in Argentina) on best original music for theater. Also, he published several books for saxophone: "SAXOPHONE STYLES",
"TANGO SOLOS FOR SAXOPHONE".

Jorge Polanuer can be reached at:
Castillo 44 dto 2
Capital Federal (1414) Buenos Aires Argentina
Tel: (5411) 4856-2133
e-mail: jorge@cuatrovientos.com.ar
http://www.cuatrovientos.com.ar

Rainy Day Waltz

In Continental Style

Written by Jorge Polanuer

Without Realizing It

Tango

Written by Jorge Polanuer

8

1920's Tango Sheet Music Cover

Pretty Buenos Aires

Tango

Music by Brian Chambouleyron

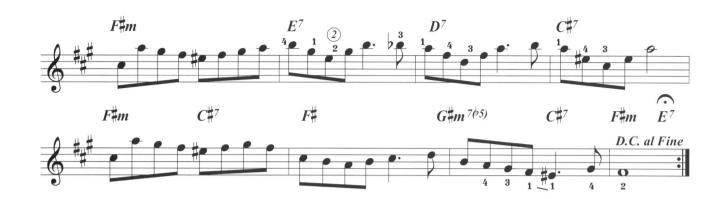

Don't Kill Me or I'll Die

Milango

Written by Jorge Polanuer

If Mama Says So

Guitar Duet

Music by Brian Chambouleyron

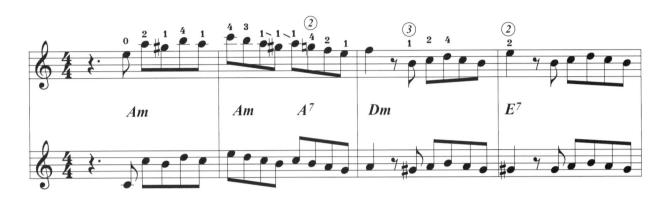

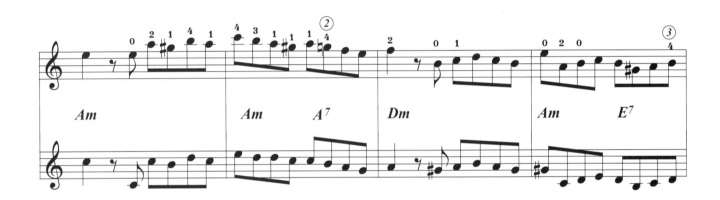

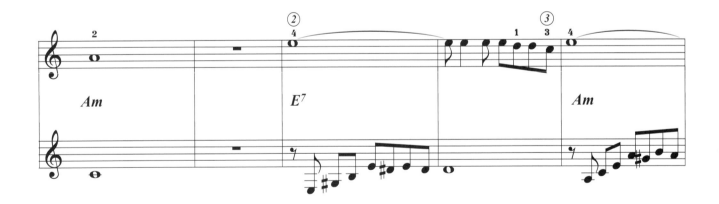

14

15

Blanca

Tango

Music by Brian Chambouleyron

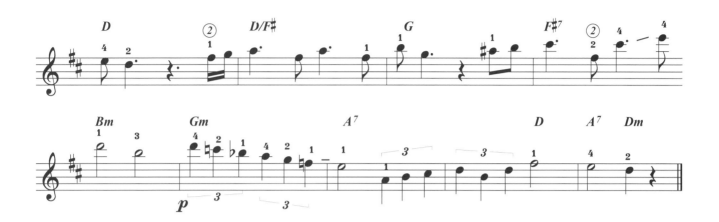

A tango event called "Glorias Portenas"
Guitarist Silvio Cattaneo on left, Brian Chambouleyron on right

17

Childhoods Memories

Waltz

Music by Brian Chambouleyron

My Friend

Tango

Music by Jorge Polanuer

It's Raining

Tango

Music by Brian Chambouleyron

Nothing to Lose

Music by Jorge Polanuer

Tango

Strolling

Tango

Music by Brian Chambouleyron

Nobody left in Town

Tango

Music by Jorge Polanuer

The Farewell Waltz

Music by Brian Chambouleyron

GUITAR INSTRUCTION & TECHNIQUE

THE GUITAR CHORD SHAPES OF CHARLIE CHRISTIAN
Book/CD Pack
by Joe Weidlich

The concepts and fingerings in this book have been developed by analyzing the licks used by Charlie Christian. Chord shapes are moveable; thus one can play the riffs in virtually any key without difficulty by simply moving the shape, and fingerings used to play them, up or down the fingerboard. The author shows how the chord shapes – F, D and A – are formed, then can easily be modified to major, minor, dominant seventh and diminished seventh chord voicings.†Analyzing licks frequently used by Charlie Christian, Joe has identified a series of what he calls tetrafragments, i.e., the core element of a lick. The identifiable "sound" of a particular lick is preserved regardless of how many notes are added on either side of it, e.g., pickup notes or tag endings.† Many examples are shown and played on the CD of how this basic concept was used by Charlie Christian to keep his solo lines moving forward. Weidlich also makes observations on the physical manner Charlie Christian used in playing jazz guitar and how that approach contributed to his smooth, mostly down stroke, pick technique.
00000388 Guitar $19.95

GUITAR CHORDS PLUS
by Ron Middlebrook

A comprehensive study of normal and extended chords, tuning, keys, transposing, capo use, and more. Includes over 500 helpful photos and diagrams, a key to guitar symbols, and a glossary of guitar terms.
00000011 ....$11.95

GUITAR TRANSCRIBING – A COMPLETE GUIDE
by Dave Celentano

Learn that solo now! Don't wait for the music to come out – use this complete guide to writing down what you hear. Includes tips, advice, examples and exercises from easy to difficult. Your ear is the top priority and you'll train it to listen more effectively to recognize intervals, chords, note values, counting rhythms and much more for an accurate transcription.
00000378 Book/CD Pack $19.95

GUITAR TUNING FOR THE COMPLETE MUSICAL IDIOT (FOR SMART PEOPLE TOO)
by Ron Middlebrook

A complete book on how to tune up. Contents include: Everything You Need To Know About Tuning; Intonation; Strings; 12-String Tuning; Picks; and much more.
00000002 ....$5.95

INTRODUCTION TO ROOTS GUITAR
by Doug Cox

This book/CD pack by Canada's premier guitar and Dobro® player introduces beginning to intermediate players to many of the basics of folk/roots guitar. Topics covered include: basic theory, tuning, reading tablature, right- and left-hand patterns, blues rhythms, Travis picking, frailing patterns, flatpicking, open tunings, slide and many more. CD includes 40 demonstration tracks.
00000262 Book/CD Pack $17.95
00000265 VHS Video $19.95

KILLER PENTATONICS FOR GUITAR
by Dave Celentano

Covers innovative and diverse ways of playing pentatonic scales in blues, rock and heavy metal. The licks and ideas in this book will give you a fresh approach to playing the pentatonic scale, hopefully inspiring you to reach for higher levels in your playing. The 37-minute companion CD features recorded examples.
00000285 Book/CD Pack $17.95

LEFT HAND GUITAR CHORD CHART
by Ron Middlebrook

Printed on durable card stock, this "first-of-a-kind" guitar chord chart displays all forms of major and minor chords in two forms, beginner and advanced.
00000005 ....$2.95

MELODIC LINES FOR THE INTERMEDIATE GUITARIST
by Greg Cooper

This book/CD pack is essential for anyone interested in expanding melodic concepts on the guitar. Author Greg Cooper covers: picking exercises; major, minor, dominant and altered lines; blues and jazz turn-arounds; and more.
00000312 Book/CD Pack $19.95

MELODY CHORDS FOR GUITAR
by Allan Holdsworth

Influential fusion player Allan Holdsworth provides guitarists with a simplified method of learning chords, in diagram form, for playing accompaniments and for playing popular melodies in "chord-solo" style. Covers: major, minor, altered, dominant and diminished scale notes in chord form, with lots of helpful reference tables and diagrams.
00000222 ....$19.95

MODAL JAMS AND THEORY
by Dave Celentano

This book shows you how to play the modes, the theory behind mode construction, how to play any mode in any key, how to play the proper mode over a given chord progression, and how to write chord progressions for each of the seven modes. The CD includes two rhythm tracks and a short solo for each mode so guitarists can practice with a "real" band.
00000163 Book/CD Pack $17.95

MONSTER SCALES AND MODES
by Dave Celentano

This book is a complete compilation of scales, modes, exotic scales, and theory. It covers the most common and exotic scales, theory on how they're constructed, and practical applications. No prior music theory knowledge is necessary, since every section is broken down and explained very clearly.
00000140 ....$7.95

OLD TIME COUNTRY GUITAR BACKUP BASICS
by Joseph Weidlich

This instructional book uses commercial recordings from 70 different "sides" from the 1920s and early 1930s as its basis to learn the principal guitar backup techniques commonly used in old-time country music. Topics covered include: boom-chick patterns • bass runs • uses of the pentatonic scale • rhythmic variations • minor chromatic nuances • the use of chromatic passing tones • licks based on chords or chord progressions • and more.
00000389 ....$15.95

OPEN GUITAR TUNINGS
by Ron Middlebrook

This booklet illustrates over 75 different tunings in easy-to-read diagrams. Includes tunings used by artists such as Chet Atkins, Michael Hedges, Jimmy Page, Joe Satriani and more for rock, blues, bluegrass, folk and country styles including open D (for slide guitar), Em, open C, modal tunings and many more.
00000130..$4.95

OPEN TUNINGS FOR GUITAR
by Dorian Michael

This book provides 14 folk songs in 9 tunings to help guitarists become comfortable with changing tunings. Songs are ordered so that changing from one tuning to another is logical and non-intrusive. Includes: Fisher Blues (DADGBE) • Fine Toast to Hewlett (DGDGBE) • George Barbazan (DGDGBD) • Amelia (DGDGCD) • Will the Circle Be Unbroken (DADF#AD) • more.
00000224 Book/CD Pack....................................$19.95

ARRANGING FOR OPEN GUITAR TUNINGS
By Dorian Michael

This book/CD pack teaches intermediate-level guitarists how to choose an appropriate tuning for a song, develop an arrangement, and solve any problems that may arise while turning a melody into a guitar piece to play and enjoy.
00000313 Book/CD Pack $19.95

ROCK RHYTHM GUITAR
by Dave Celentano

This helpful book/CD pack cuts out all the confusing technical talk and just gives guitarists the essential tools to get them playing. With Celentano's tips, anyone can build a solid foundation of basic skills to play almost any rhythm guitar style. The exercises and examples are on the CD, in order of difficulty, so players can master new techniques, then move on to more challenging material.
00000274 Book/CD Pack $17.95

SCALES AND MODES IN THE BEGINNING
by Ron Middlebrook

The most comprehensive and complete scale book written especially for the guitar. Chapers include: Fretboard Visualization • Scale Terminology • Scales and Modes • and a Scale to Chord Guide.
00000010..$11.95

SLIDE GUITAR AND OPEN TUNINGS
by Doug Cox

Explores the basics of open tunings and slide guitar for the intermediate player, including licks, chords, songs and patterns. This is not just a repertoire book, but rather an approach for guitarists to jam with others, invent their own songs, and understand how to find their way around open tunings with and without a slide. The accompanying CD features 37 tracks.
00000243 Book/CD Pack $17.95

SPEED METAL
by Dave Celentano

In an attempt to teach the aspiring rock guitarist how to pick faster and play more melodically, Dave Celentano uses heavy metal neo-classical styles from Paganini and Bach to rock in this great book/CD pack. The book is structured to take the player through the examples in order of difficulty.
00000261 Book/CD Pack $17.95

25 WAYS TO IMPROVE YOUR SOLO GUITAR PLAYING
by Jay Marks

Keep your music fresh with the great ideas in this new book! Covers: chords, dynamics, harmonics, phrasing, intros & endings and more!
00000323 Book/CD Pack $19.95

Centerstream Publishing, LLC
P.O Box 17878 - Anaheim Hills, CA 92817
P/Fax (714)-779-9390 - Email: Centerstream@aol.com
Website: www.centerstream-usa.com